EMMANUEL JOSEPH

Gameful Wisdom, How Play and Learning Unlock Spiritual Enlightenment

Copyright © 2025 by Emmanuel Joseph

All rights reserved. No part of this publication may be reproduced, stored or transmitted in any form or by any means, electronic, mechanical, photocopying, recording, scanning, or otherwise without written permission from the publisher. It is illegal to copy this book, post it to a website, or distribute it by any other means without permission.

First edition

This book was professionally typeset on Reedsy.
Find out more at reedsy.com

Contents

1	Chapter 1: The Essence of Play	1
2	Chapter 2: The Intersection of Play and Learning	3
3	Chapter 3: Spiritual Insights from Play	5
4	Chapter 4: The Role of Games in Spiritual Practice	7
5	Chapter 5: Mindfulness and Play	9
6	Chapter 6: Creativity and Innovation Through Play	11
7	Chapter 7: Building Resilience Through Play	13
8	Chapter 8: Play and Social Connection	15
9	Chapter 9: Play in Adulthood	17
10	Chapter 10: Play and Personal Growth	19
11	Chapter 11: Creating a Playful Culture	21
12	Chapter 12: Embracing Gameful Wisdom	23
13	Chapter 13: The Healing Power of Play	25
14	Chapter 14: The Wisdom of Childlike Wonder	26
15	Chapter 15: The Future of Play and Learning	27

1

Chapter 1: The Essence of Play

Play is often dismissed as mere frivolity, something to indulge in only when the serious work of life is done. Yet, play is much more than a simple escape from reality. At its core, play is a profound exploration of self and the world around us. Through play, we unlock creativity, spontaneity, and joy. Play allows us to access a deeper state of being, where we are free to experiment, take risks, and learn without the fear of failure. This chapter explores the fundamental nature of play and its intrinsic value in human life.

In the act of play, we enter a state of flow, where time seems to stand still and our worries fade into the background. This state of flow is characterized by deep immersion and enjoyment, often leading to a heightened sense of fulfillment. Whether it's the simple joy of a child playing with a toy or the complex strategies of an adult engaged in a board game, play provides an avenue for experiencing life in its purest form.

The benefits of play extend beyond personal enjoyment. Research has shown that play can improve cognitive function, enhance problem-solving skills, and promote emotional well-being. Play stimulates the brain, encouraging neural connections that support creativity and innovation. It also fosters social connections, as people often engage in play together, building bonds and strengthening relationships.

Play is not limited to childhood; it is a lifelong necessity. Adults who engage in play report higher levels of happiness and reduced stress. Play can take many forms, from sports and hobbies to imaginative activities and games. By embracing play throughout our lives, we can maintain a sense of wonder and curiosity, continuously exploring new possibilities and perspectives.

2

Chapter 2: The Intersection of Play and Learning

Learning and play are often seen as separate domains—one serious, the other lighthearted. However, when these two elements merge, they create a powerful synergy. Playful learning harnesses the natural curiosity and engagement that comes with play to facilitate deeper understanding and retention of knowledge. By making learning enjoyable and immersive, we can break down barriers to education and make it accessible to all. This chapter delves into the ways in which play enhances learning and how we can integrate playfulness into educational systems.

When we engage in playful learning, we tap into a state of intrinsic motivation. Unlike traditional education methods that rely on external rewards, playful learning encourages a love of discovery for its own sake. This intrinsic motivation fuels a deeper engagement with the material, leading to a more profound and lasting understanding. For example, games and simulations can make complex concepts more tangible and relatable, allowing learners to grasp abstract ideas through hands-on experience.

Furthermore, playful learning promotes a growth mindset, where mistakes are viewed as opportunities for growth rather than failures. In the context of play, the fear of failure is diminished, and learners feel more comfortable taking risks and experimenting with new ideas. This mindset encourages resilience and perseverance, which are crucial traits for lifelong learning. By embracing the playful aspect of learning, we create an environment where students feel empowered to explore and innovate.

The benefits of playful learning extend beyond the classroom. In the workplace, fostering a playful attitude can enhance creativity, teamwork, and problem-solving skills. Companies that encourage a culture of play often see increased employee satisfaction and productivity. Playful learning can also be a powerful tool for social change, as it can be used to raise awareness and engage communities in addressing societal issues. By integrating play into various aspects of our lives, we can create a more dynamic and inclusive learning experience.

Playful learning is not just a trend; it is a fundamental shift in how we approach education. By recognizing the importance of play in learning, we can transform our educational systems to better meet the needs of all learners. This chapter has highlighted the ways in which play can enhance learning and provided insights into how we can incorporate playfulness into our educational practices.

3

Chapter 3: Spiritual Insights from Play

Play is not just a tool for learning; it is also a gateway to spiritual enlightenment. In moments of play, we experience a sense of timelessness and flow, where the boundaries between self and the universe blur. Play connects us to our inner child, a part of us that is pure and unencumbered by the stresses of daily life. This chapter explores how play can lead to spiritual insights and awakenings, guiding us on a path to greater self-awareness and connection with the divine.

When we engage in play, we often enter a state of flow where we lose track of time and become fully immersed in the activity. This state of flow is similar to the meditative state achieved through spiritual practices, allowing us to transcend the ordinary and tap into a higher consciousness. Play provides a space where we can explore our deepest desires, fears, and aspirations in a safe and non-judgmental environment.

Furthermore, play fosters a sense of joy and wonder that is essential for spiritual growth. In play, we experience moments of pure happiness and laughter, which open our hearts and minds to the beauty and mystery of life. This joy is a powerful force that can dissolve negative emotions and elevate our spirits, helping us to cultivate a positive and grateful attitude.

Play also encourages us to embrace our authentic selves. In play, we are free to express our true nature without fear of judgment or criticism. This authenticity is a cornerstone of spiritual enlightenment, as it allows us to connect with our inner truth and live in alignment with our higher purpose. Through play, we can uncover hidden aspects of ourselves and gain insights that lead to greater self-awareness and spiritual awakening.

4

Chapter 4: The Role of Games in Spiritual Practice

Games have long been a part of spiritual traditions across cultures. From the strategic moves of chess to the contemplative steps of a labyrinth, games offer a structured way to engage with spiritual concepts and practices. They provide a safe space to explore ethical dilemmas, develop patience and resilience, and cultivate a sense of community. This chapter examines various games and their roles in spiritual practice, highlighting the lessons they impart and the wisdom they unveil.

Chess, for example, has been used as a metaphor for the human struggle between good and evil, with each move representing a decision that shapes one's destiny. The game teaches strategic thinking, patience, and the importance of considering the long-term consequences of our actions. Similarly, labyrinths are used in meditation and prayer, guiding individuals on a journey of self-discovery and contemplation. Walking a labyrinth can help quiet the mind and open the heart to divine guidance.

Traditional board games and card games also offer opportunities for spiritual growth. These games often involve themes of cooperation, competition, and ethical decision-making, which mirror the challenges we face in our spiritual journeys. By engaging in these games, we can reflect on our values, develop virtues such as honesty and humility, and strengthen our connections with others.

In addition to traditional games, modern video games can also serve as tools for spiritual practice. Many video games incorporate themes of heroism, sacrifice, and redemption, providing a virtual space to explore spiritual concepts. Games that emphasize cooperation and teamwork can foster a sense of community and shared purpose, while those that challenge players to overcome obstacles can teach resilience and perseverance.

5

Chapter 5: Mindfulness and Play

Mindfulness is the practice of being fully present in the moment, a state often achieved through meditation. However, play can also be a powerful vehicle for mindfulness. When we engage in play, we immerse ourselves fully in the activity, paying close attention to our actions and surroundings. This chapter discusses how play can enhance mindfulness, helping us to cultivate a deeper awareness of the present moment and reduce stress and anxiety.

In play, we often find ourselves completely absorbed in the task at hand, whether it's solving a puzzle, playing a sport, or creating art. This focused attention is a key aspect of mindfulness, as it allows us to connect with the present moment and let go of distracting thoughts. By practicing mindfulness through play, we can train our minds to stay present and develop a greater sense of clarity and calm.

Play also encourages us to engage our senses fully, which is another important element of mindfulness. Whether it's the feel of a ball in our hands, the sound of laughter, or the sight of colorful game pieces, play invites us to experience the world with heightened awareness. This sensory engagement helps ground us in the present moment and deepens our connection to the here and now.

Furthermore, play can help us approach mindfulness with a sense of lightness and ease. While traditional mindfulness practices can sometimes feel rigid or serious, play brings an element of fun and spontaneity. This playful approach can make mindfulness more accessible and enjoyable, encouraging us to incorporate it into our daily lives.

6

Chapter 6: Creativity and Innovation Through Play

Play stimulates our imagination and encourages us to think outside the box. It fosters an environment where new ideas can flourish and where we feel free to experiment without fear of judgment. Many of the world's greatest innovations have emerged from a playful mindset. This chapter explores the relationship between play and creativity, offering insights into how we can harness play to drive innovation and problem-solving in various fields.

When we engage in play, we often find ourselves thinking in unconventional ways, making connections between seemingly unrelated ideas, and exploring new possibilities. This creative thinking is essential for innovation, as it allows us to break free from traditional patterns and discover novel solutions. By embracing a playful mindset, we can unlock our creative potential and approach challenges with fresh perspectives.

Play also provides a safe space for experimentation and risk-taking. In play, failure is not seen as a setback but as a valuable part of the learning process. This willingness to take risks and learn from mistakes is crucial for innovation, as it encourages us to explore new ideas without fear of judgment. By creating an environment where play is encouraged, we can foster a culture of innovation and continuous improvement.

Furthermore, play can enhance our ability to collaborate and work effectively with others. Many forms of play, from team sports to collaborative games, require us to communicate, cooperate, and build on each other's ideas. This collaborative spirit is essential for innovation, as it allows us to leverage diverse perspectives and strengths to achieve common goals. By fostering a playful and inclusive culture, we can drive creativity and innovation in our organizations and communities.

7

Chapter 7: Building Resilience Through Play

Life is filled with challenges and setbacks, and building resilience is key to navigating these obstacles. Play teaches us to be adaptable and resilient, as it often involves overcoming challenges and dealing with unexpected outcomes. Through play, we learn to embrace failure as a part of the learning process and to approach difficulties with a positive and open mindset. This chapter examines how play helps build resilience and how we can apply these lessons to our daily lives.

In play, we frequently encounter situations where things don't go as planned. Whether it's losing a game, facing a tough opponent, or solving a difficult puzzle, play challenges us to think on our feet and adapt to changing circumstances. These experiences teach us valuable lessons about perseverance, patience, and the importance of maintaining a positive attitude even in the face of adversity.

Play also encourages a sense of experimentation and risk-taking, which are essential components of resilience. When we play, we are more willing to take risks and try new things, knowing that the stakes are low and the potential for growth is high. This willingness to step outside our comfort zones and embrace uncertainty helps us develop the mental and emotional flexibility needed to cope with life's challenges.

Moreover, play provides a safe space to process and express emotions. Through play, we can explore and release feelings of frustration, anger, and disappointment in a healthy and constructive way. This emotional regulation is a key aspect of resilience, as it allows us to manage our emotions effectively and maintain a balanced perspective in difficult situations.

8

Chapter 8: Play and Social Connection

Humans are inherently social beings, and play is a powerful way to foster social connections. Whether it's through team sports, board games, or collaborative projects, play brings people together and strengthens bonds. It teaches us important social skills such as communication, cooperation, and empathy. This chapter explores the social benefits of play and how it can be used to build stronger, more connected communities.

Play provides a natural setting for social interaction, as it often involves collaboration, competition, and shared experiences. Through play, we learn to communicate effectively, negotiate, and work together towards common goals. These social skills are crucial for building and maintaining healthy relationships, both in our personal and professional lives.

In addition to fostering social skills, play also promotes empathy and understanding. When we engage in play with others, we gain insights into their perspectives, feelings, and motivations. This increased empathy helps us build deeper connections and foster a sense of belonging and community. By playing together, we create shared memories and experiences that strengthen our bonds and create lasting friendships.

Furthermore, play can be a powerful tool for social change. Games and playful activities can raise awareness, promote dialogue, and engage communities in addressing important social issues. By harnessing the power of play, we can create inclusive and supportive environments that encourage positive social interactions and community building.

9

Chapter 9: Play in Adulthood

While play is often associated with childhood, its benefits extend well into adulthood. Adults who engage in play report higher levels of happiness, reduced stress, and improved cognitive function. Play can also reignite a sense of wonder and curiosity that often diminishes with age. This chapter discusses the importance of maintaining a playful attitude throughout life and offers practical ways for adults to incorporate play into their routines.

As we grow older, the demands of work, family, and daily responsibilities can often lead us to neglect play. However, incorporating play into our lives can have significant benefits for our mental, emotional, and physical well-being. Engaging in playful activities helps reduce stress, boost mood, and enhance cognitive function, making us more resilient and better equipped to handle life's challenges.

Play also encourages a sense of exploration and creativity, which are essential for personal growth and fulfillment. By embracing a playful attitude, we can approach life with a sense of curiosity and open-mindedness, continually seeking new experiences and opportunities for growth. This mindset helps us stay engaged and motivated, preventing stagnation and burnout.

There are many ways for adults to incorporate play into their lives, from pursuing hobbies and sports to participating in social games and activities.

The key is to find activities that bring joy and relaxation, allowing us to reconnect with our inner child and experience the many benefits of play. By making play a regular part of our routines, we can maintain a sense of balance and well-being throughout our lives.

10

Chapter 10: Play and Personal Growth

Personal growth is a lifelong journey, and play can be a valuable companion on this path. Through play, we discover new interests, develop skills, and gain insights into our own behaviors and motivations. Play challenges us to step outside our comfort zones and embrace new experiences. This chapter examines how play contributes to personal growth and provides strategies for using play to achieve our personal and professional goals.

When we engage in play, we often find ourselves exploring new activities and interests that we might not have considered before. This exploration helps us discover new passions and talents, broadening our horizons and enriching our lives. By trying new things and taking on new challenges, we develop a deeper understanding of ourselves and our capabilities.

Play also provides opportunities for skill development and mastery. Whether it's learning a new sport, playing a musical instrument, or solving puzzles, play allows us to practice and hone our skills in a fun and engaging way. This skill development not only enhances our abilities but also boosts our confidence and self-esteem, empowering us to pursue our goals with greater determination.

Furthermore, play offers valuable insights into our behaviors and motivations. Through play, we can observe our reactions to different situations, identify patterns in our thinking and behavior, and gain a deeper understanding of our strengths and areas for growth. This self-awareness is a crucial aspect of personal growth, as it enables us to make more informed choices and take proactive steps towards self-improvement.

11

Chapter 11: Creating a Playful Culture

For play to be truly transformative, it must be embraced at both individual and societal levels. Creating a culture that values play involves rethinking our attitudes toward work, education, and leisure. It requires us to recognize the benefits of play and to design environments that encourage playful behavior. This chapter explores how we can foster a culture of play in our homes, schools, workplaces, and communities.

Creating a playful culture starts with changing our perceptions of play. Rather than viewing play as a frivolous or unproductive activity, we need to recognize its intrinsic value and its potential to enhance our well-being and personal growth. By shifting our attitudes toward play, we can create environments that encourage and celebrate playful behavior.

In schools, integrating play into the curriculum can create more engaging and effective learning experiences. By incorporating games, creative activities, and experiential learning, educators can foster a love of learning and help students develop essential skills and knowledge. Similarly, workplaces that embrace play can boost employee morale, creativity, and productivity, creating a more dynamic and innovative work environment.

Communities can also play a role in promoting a culture of play by providing spaces and opportunities for people of all ages to engage in playful activities. Parks, recreational centers, and community events can create a sense of connection and belonging, fostering stronger, more cohesive communities. By prioritizing play in our public spaces and policies, we can create a more inclusive and supportive society.

12

Chapter 12: Embracing Gameful Wisdom

Gameful wisdom is the understanding that play and learning are not just activities but ways of being. It is the recognition that play can lead to profound spiritual and personal growth and that learning can be a joyful and engaging process. Embracing gameful wisdom means integrating play into our daily lives and allowing it to guide us toward enlightenment. This final chapter offers reflections on the journey of gameful wisdom and provides practical tips for living a playfully enlightened life.

To embrace gameful wisdom, we need to cultivate a mindset that values play and learning as integral parts of our existence. This involves being open to new experiences, approaching life with curiosity and wonder, and finding joy in the process of discovery. By adopting this playful mindset, we can navigate life's challenges with greater resilience and creativity, continually seeking opportunities for growth and enlightenment.

Incorporating play into our daily routines can also help us live more fulfilling and balanced lives. Whether it's setting aside time for hobbies, engaging in playful activities with friends and family, or finding ways to make our work more enjoyable, integrating play into our lives can enhance our well-being and personal growth.

Ultimately, gameful wisdom is about finding harmony between play and learning, and recognizing that both are essential for a meaningful and enlightened life. By embracing this wisdom, we can unlock our full potential, cultivate deeper connections with ourselves and others, and embark on a journey of continuous growth and discovery.

13

Chapter 13: The Healing Power of Play

Play has remarkable healing properties that can help us recover from emotional and psychological wounds. Engaging in play allows us to access a state of joy and relaxation, which can counteract the effects of stress and trauma. This chapter delves into the therapeutic benefits of play, exploring how it can be used as a tool for healing and recovery.

Therapeutic play is often used in mental health treatment to help individuals process their emotions and experiences. Activities such as art therapy, drama therapy, and play therapy provide a safe space for individuals to express themselves creatively and work through difficult feelings. Through play, individuals can gain insights into their emotional states, develop coping strategies, and build resilience.

Moreover, play can help restore a sense of normalcy and stability in the aftermath of traumatic events. It offers a way to reconnect with the present moment and find solace in the simple pleasures of life. By incorporating play into our healing journeys, we can nurture our emotional well-being and promote recovery.

14

Chapter 14: The Wisdom of Childlike Wonder

Childlike wonder is a state of awe and curiosity that allows us to see the world with fresh eyes. It is characterized by an openness to new experiences and a sense of delight in the ordinary. This chapter explores the wisdom of childlike wonder and how we can cultivate this mindset to enrich our lives and deepen our spiritual practice.

Children naturally approach the world with a sense of wonder, finding joy in the simplest things and asking questions with boundless curiosity. As adults, we often lose this sense of wonder, becoming bogged down by routine and responsibilities. However, by reconnecting with our inner child, we can rediscover the magic in everyday life and open ourselves to new possibilities.

Cultivating childlike wonder involves embracing a mindset of curiosity and playfulness. It means allowing ourselves to be surprised by the world, seeking out new experiences, and approaching life with a sense of adventure. By doing so, we can infuse our lives with joy and excitement, and deepen our connection to the present moment.

15

Chapter 15: The Future of Play and Learning

As we look to the future, the role of play in learning and personal growth will continue to evolve. Advances in technology, changes in societal attitudes, and a growing recognition of the importance of play will shape how we integrate play into our lives. This chapter explores the future of play and learning, examining emerging trends and their potential impact on our well-being and spiritual development.

Technology has the potential to revolutionize the way we engage in play and learning. Virtual reality, augmented reality, and gamification are just a few examples of how technology can create immersive and interactive experiences that enhance our understanding and enjoyment of the world. These innovations can make learning more engaging and accessible, providing new opportunities for exploration and creativity.

Additionally, there is a growing movement to prioritize play and well-being in education and the workplace. Schools and organizations are increasingly recognizing the value of play in fostering creativity, collaboration, and resilience. As we continue to embrace these principles, we can create environments that support holistic development and lifelong learning.

The future of play and learning is bright, with endless possibilities for growth and innovation. By staying open to new ideas and approaches, we can harness the power of play to unlock our full potential and lead more fulfilling, enlightened lives.

Book Title: Gameful Wisdom: How Play and Learning Unlock Spiritual Enlightenment

Book Description:

In "Gameful Wisdom," embark on a transformative journey where play and learning intertwine to unlock profound spiritual enlightenment. This enlightening book reveals the hidden power of play, offering readers a fresh perspective on how playful activities can lead to deep personal and spiritual growth.

Through twelve captivating chapters, you'll explore the essence of play and its intrinsic value in human life. Discover how playful learning fosters creativity, resilience, and social connections, making education and personal growth more engaging and enjoyable. Uncover the spiritual insights gained through play, and learn how games from various traditions can serve as powerful tools for spiritual practice.

Delve into the therapeutic benefits of play and how it aids in healing emotional wounds and promoting well-being. Embrace the wisdom of childlike wonder, reigniting a sense of awe and curiosity in everyday life. The book also looks toward the future, examining emerging trends and technological advancements that will shape the way we play and learn.

With practical tips and profound reflections, "Gameful Wisdom" encourages readers to integrate play into their daily lives, creating a harmonious balance between joy, learning, and enlightenment. Whether you're a lifelong learner, a spiritual seeker, or simply someone looking to infuse more joy into your life, this book offers a unique and insightful guide to the transformative power of play.

www.ingramcontent.com/pod-product-compliance
Lightning Source LLC
LaVergne TN
LVHW020740090526
838202LV00057BA/6146